Spiritual Atheist

MAKING SENSE OF LIFE, SCIENCE, RELIGION, AND ATHEISM

PETER AHKIA

AHKIA INSTITUTE

"Imagine there is no heaven, no hell below us, above us only sky."

– John Lennon, *Imagine*

"We are words in a sentence,

Dancing,

In the poem of life"

– Peter Ahkia

Published by Ahkia Institute. www.ahkia.com

eBook: 979-8-9897895-2-8

Paperback: 979-8-9897895-1-1

Hardback: 979-8-9897895-0-4

Contents

Foreword

One early morning, I dreamt of a life where I had a daughter, and we were having a conversation about coffee. Being a light sleeper, I am normally a non-coffee drinker, but, much like my taste for wine, I do enjoy all sorts of natural food ingredients and tastes. My solution to this dilemma is decaf coffee. Of course, my teenage daughter did not approve, speaking of how caffeine is part of the taste—the same argument that my friends make with a cringe whenever I drink non-alcoholic anything.

The conversation led to a discussion about whether decaf coffee is still coffee. It dawned on me the similarity between this seemingly casual discussion of no grand significance to the title of this book, which I wondered for alternatives that would be the right fit.

To me, the topic of "spirituality" had always been the central message of the book from the beginning, and, from the perspective of the broader human experience, "religion," "atheism," and "science" all follow closely after "spirituality" as contextual fields within which we can discuss spirituality.

What, then, is the key ingredient? We are tempted to think that caffeine is the defining ingredient in coffee, but that is only one ingredient. But if I, like millions of others who drink coffee, can still enjoy coffee in its decaf form, what we are drinking in the decaffeinated form is still coffee. In the end, perhaps water, which is the essence of life, is the key ingredient we serve, and the objective is to have a drink of any kind, and not necessarily coffee or tea or wine. I will leave it for you to decide whether this analogy serves you in your own understanding of the remaining content of the book.

For me, this little dream excursion solidified the title, setting it apart from the original possible titles of *Spiritual Atheism*, *Atheist Perspective of Spiritualism*, or *Atheist Spirituality*. It became clear that the title needed to be *Spiritual Atheist*. In the end, spirituality is about life itself. We can choose to have the terminology or our belief about the word "God" as part of the equation of spirituality or not. In the end, the word "God" has no meaning other than the meaning we give it. We are living and we are life itself. We can argue about the means of our existence, our origin, our understanding, our purpose, and whether there is any supreme being that governs us. But that which we are—life—simply is.

Introduction

This book is, first and foremost, about spirituality. I accept the definition that spirituality is about life itself. In essence, nothing is not by nature spiritual. Therefore, it must be that spirituality has to do with religion (theology) and atheism alike. Indeed, spirituality pertains to the truth of "what is so" and the practice based on the truth of "what works." In this regard, whether one believes in the existence of God (the definition of whether one is religious or an atheist) becomes irrelevant in spirituality. Furthermore, because spirituality is about the truth of life, it embraces science and religion for as long as they express truth.

The truth discussed in this book is what I believe to be true. I also believe one can truly know the truth without being absolutely certain of it. It is like we can know it in our hearts to be true even though we lack proof. Moreover, I hold the unusual belief that, as long as something works, we can adopt it as our operative belief without ever needing absolute proof. That does not mean we intentionally delude ourselves—we use proof, evidence, credibility, and experience to tell us the possible truths whenever possible to assist us in our understanding of all of existence. But these methods of arriving at possible truths are no substitute for our inner awareness and attunement to absolute truth. Nor are they excuses, where proof is absent using these methods, that we use to shrug our shoulders to say that we simply do not know or worse, that such truth simply cannot be known.

We can always choose to believe in something or nothing at all. Such choice makes our reality and, therefore, is our truth no matter the reality of universal truth. In the absence of proof, we go by what we believe is true and what works, and we move on until new information tells us otherwise. In this eternal dance of knowing and adjusting, we go through the universe as babies, marveling and creating the world around us. We are truly a species of such imagination that we can imagine anything into being.

CHAPTER 1

What does an atheist believe?

Consider, if you will, that there is no heaven or hell, no afterlife. There is only "what is." This pretty much sums up what an atheist believes—plus all the permutations of believing in a combination of scientific theories of the Big Bang, quantum physics, and some notion of time and space as current scientific theories define them. I will use this atheistic belief system as the basis of discussing spirituality in this book and make the case that atheism can be one path to spiritual mastery.

The only thing I ask of you as my audience is for you to keep an open mind. My hope is that by the end of the book, you will draw your own conclusion and form a belief system that serves you. If you continue to adopt your current religious beliefs or non-beliefs, hopefully, you can come to them with a new take that serves you and improves your understanding of life.

Yes, I certainly hope people of religion will be in touch with the materials discussed here somehow, perhaps to embrace it, question it, debunk it, tear it apart, or call it blasphemy. That is all fine. I simply point to one way, one thinking, with the only simple agenda being that you will form your own conclusion about all of it.

CHAPTER 2

The "what is"

What is the so-called "what is"? We can also call that "all of it," which is everything that is manifested and unmanifested in our existence. What is the biggest thing you can think of that can describe our collective existence? Start with yourself being one person, then your family, the human society at large, the planet, the solar system, the galaxy, and the universe. Most people stop here with the physical description of existence. Perhaps some people will add further ingredients, such as all the matter and energy within the universe (dark matter and dark energy included), multiple dimensions (whatever that describes, whether it is based on string theory or more esoteric new age beliefs), multiverse, and all possible versions thereof (possibility-probability matrix). Some spiritual thinkers even add "the unmanifest-ed" to cover everything that cannot be described.

Fair enough. Feel free to think up anything that is not yet covered above and throw it in there. I humbly suggest here that the collection of descriptions you end up using can be described as "what is, what was, and what will be." Alternatively, we can call that "the manifested and the unmanifested" (whether unmanifested means whatever existed that no longer exists or whatever does not exist now but shall exist later). Ultimately, if I may use our limited human language to simply give it one word, it would be "All" (I will use this capitalized form for the rest of the book), to mean all that you can think of as the largest existence (and beyond).

CHAPTER 3

You have always existed and will always exist

O nce we have this notion of All, let us think about our existence within that context. Do you believe that you are part of this existence? I believe most people would answer the affirmative. Then, do you believe you have existed in some form since the "beginning," whenever that may be (Big Bang, pre-Big Bang)? A certain number of you may come to the conclusion of "yes," because that can simply mean the atoms that make up who you are at the physical level have existed since the beginning.

Most physics theories say that energy can neither be created nor destroyed; it can only change form, which must mean that all energy must have existed since the beginning of time. Therefore, "you" must have existed at the energy level as well as the physical level since the beginning.

Alternatively, another question you might ask is whether what makes up "you" will continue to exist after our understanding of the so-called death, since energy can neither be created nor destroyed. Perhaps most of you can accept that the energy part of "you" will continue to exist forever, although in different forms.

CHAPTER 4

The essence of who you are

If most people can understand that the physical and energetic composition of "you" has always existed and always will be. What about the part that makes "you" who you are as you understand it practically? Surely, it is fine to accept that you have existed since the beginning of time as atoms or energy and will continue to exist. However, the "you" now is not of the same collection of specific atoms because, as we shed skin, circulate, digest, and rejuvenate, we are not exactly the same physical composition as the previous minute, hour, day, month, or year. What, then, makes up "you"? Perhaps we can, for the time being, call whatever gives "you" an identifiable, practical, and functional existence "consciousness." This consciousness allows you to be aware of yourself, recognize yourself and others, think, feel, and do. We can also call this consciousness the true essence of your being.

Considering what we have discussed thus far, science and spirituality agree, at least in one form of spirituality.

What, then, is this "consciousness" that is the essence of your being? Where did it come from? This is where science does not quite have a confident or concrete answer. One thing we can agree on is that this consciousness is obviously intelligent and self-aware. There is also a certain permanence to it that is beyond your physical formation to an extent. For instance, when you have a heart transplant, "you" are still "you". So, your physical heart likely does not make up the essence of your being. When it comes to the natural metabolic process, your body replaces much of each of its parts over time, although some parts are replaced very slowly.

Could the brain be that which is "consciousness"? Beyond this point is where spirituality picks up after science. I will describe in deterministic terms as if the beliefs that follow are the absolute truth. They are indeed what I believe to be true, but as with anything and anyone, I could be wrong about it all.

It would be advisable to use your own discernment and decide your beliefs for yourself. All I am asking is that you keep an open mind and see the entire system of belief first before coming to a conclusion to embrace it or rebuke it (or any part therein). You can then decide for yourself what you believe to be the truth.

CHAPTER 5

We are all connected

Where science ends and spirituality picks up—for now—is the nature of this "consciousness" that is self-aware, intelligent, and makes up the essence of each human being. For an atheist, it might be palatable and somewhat acceptable to use the term "life," "life itself," or "life essence" to describe what we call "consciousness." The next leap would be to decide whether you believe your "life essence" is connected with anything beyond your physical presence or body.

Each person, at some level, has experienced a feeling of interconnectedness with that which is outside the physical self at some point in their life. When witnessing the pure joy of a child singing, observing the morning dew on a flower, feeling compassion for someone else, gazing up into the sky and looking at the stars, or the awe of realization that we are all made of the same stuff as stars—these are just some examples of how people glimpse and feel the notion that we are all connected to each other and everything around us. From this connectedness, we glimpse the truth of the oneness of All.

CHAPTER 6

Why atheists may reject religion

Although atheism is defined in most dictionaries as a lack of belief in "god," most people who hold atheistic beliefs, if they truly reflect on their beliefs, would likely describe their belief in comparison to religious beliefs. More precisely, they would likely describe how they cannot identify with any of the religious beliefs out there, and hence, come to the conclusion that there is no god (or God). In essence, an atheist likely lacks a belief in God because no religion has provided a satisfactory concept of God that an atheist can bring themselves to embrace. Therefore, a portion of atheists may not reject the belief in God as much as they reject most religions' beliefs about God.

Let us take a moment to demonstrate some possible reasons for such a pattern of beliefs in atheists in the context of what they seem to reject of certain aspects of certain religions.

A. Certain religions' staunch beliefs are counter to modern scientific discoveries. These include the belief that the Earth is only a couple thousand years old when carbon dating of fossil records clearly shows the Earth to be a few billion years old. Other examples include the denial of evolution and, previously, geocentrism (the belief that Earth is the center of the solar system, which most religions have abandoned now).

B. Certain religious teachings say they are based on love but advocate practices of exclusion, fear, violence, or hatred. These include the teachings of:

1. a certain form of elitism, such as a particular country or ethnic group being favored by God or that homosexuality is wrong. Is God not sup-

posed to be all-loving, according to many religions? Are we not all equal in the eyes of God?

2. acceptable violent activities toward certain groups, such as legitimizing the killing of non-believers in their holy scripture or everyday religious teachings. Are we not supposed to love each other unconditionally? Are we not all brothers and sisters, according to many religions?

3. acceptable (or even compulsory) practices of genital mutilation of any kind, male or female. Are we not supposed to love and care for our God-given bodies, according to many religions? What about harming others, even our babies, without their consent?

These teachings and practices of some religions seem to contradict other teachings within the same religion, not to mention running counter to some basic common sense or people's sense of right or wrong. These contradictions make it hard for some people within the religion, and especially for those outside the religion (including atheists), to take other teachings in that religion seriously as absolute truths.

C. Many religions say that God gave us free will, but then talk about punishment and eternal damnation if we do not comply with God's wishes. The concept that God gave us free will but punishes us with eternal damnation for making certain choices is logically confounding. There is no true free will if choosing one thing leads to damnation and punishment. Most religions portray an angry God that punishes, judges, and condemns humans for certain behavior while also preaching a God of love. Yet this love, by definition, cannot be true if it is conditional on certain behavior.

Logically, it also does not make sense that God—who is all-powerful—would ever need to punish, judge, or condemn people. This implies that God's creation, in God's own eyes, is somehow imperfect, so some "corrective" measures are required. But if God is all-powerful, and most religious people would agree that God is perfect, why would God's creation be imperfect? And if God truly wanted humans to behave a certain way, is God such an inferior God that God cannot get us to do what God desires? If God simply desires us to have free choice, would that not render the act of free will of any kind an expression of perfection itself? In that case, why punish us for a choice that God would not prefer? What is the point of God having any preference at all and then for us to "freely" choose?

Most confounding, what purpose does it serve God to put people through eternal damnation? For some kind of sadistic joy? This belief system simply does not make sense to many people, atheists or religious people alike. The difference is that some religious people simply set it aside as that which is unknowable or simply ignore it and pick and choose partial belief systems within a particular religion. In contrast, atheists tend to reject religion altogether because of the lack of cohesion in these God arguments and logic.

D. Insistence on religious texts being the word of God. Many religious texts, when we look at them from our present-day knowledge, are simply inaccurate (*i.e.*

the age of the Earth). Many atheists who otherwise may have embraced other parts of the teachings feel inclined to reject them because they feel that the sacred texts have been elevated to a status where they cannot be disputed—even for obvious inaccuracies. Therefore, people who disagree with any part of a sacred text must adopt it wholly or reject it altogether. Many atheists cannot comprehend why we cannot simply treat these texts as having been written by humans, with the same fallacies as any scientific text, and subject them to rigorous scientific inquiry. For, if the truth is the truth, then it should stand the test of time, let alone the test of scientific inquiry.

**

The list of why many atheists reject religion goes on and on. Some people (both atheists and people of religion) finally give up and resort to ignorance, where they say that the truth of God is unknowable. Some religions even state that seeking such knowledge is against the will of God. The non-religious counterpart of this belief is called agnosticism, which is the view that any ultimate reality (such as God) is unknown and probably unknowable.

I will acknowledge here that some atheists truly reject any notion of the existence of God. I would argue though the notion of "God" that they reject, by and large, is that of a God who exhibits some form of human behavior and human needs. I would audaciously guess that given a different definition of God or removing any preconceived notion of God as religions define God, many open minded atheists may indeed accept the possibility that some form of higher power exists. What is left, then, would be atheists who truly rebuke any existence of consciousness beyond that of humans or extraterrestrial intelligence (if they believe in the existence of extraterrestrial intelligence).

Let us neither assume or rebuke the existence of any higher power for the time being. We will revisit this concept toward the end of this book.

CHAPTER 7

Where religion is helpful

As much as many atheists reject religious doctrines that are fear-based, many atheists seem to embrace references about love in religion. Moreover, there is at least respect for the original inspirers of the religions. Notice here that I did not say "founders" of religions. There is a joke with some truth to it, which says that Mohamed was not a Muslim, Jesus was not a Christian, the Buddha was not a Buddhist, and Lao Zi (Lao Tzu) was not a Daoist (Taoist). Most religions came about *after* the death of the original inspirers. Many atheists do agree with much of the philosophy and sometimes the theologies of the original inspirers. To many atheists, the stories (true histories) of the original inspirers are as inspiring and useful as biographies and autobiographies of great historical and contemporary figures. These original inspirers not only imparted messages most human beings can identify with, but also *were* the messages of truth and practical wisdom that transcends any religion. For example:

- Lao Zi spoke of the oneness of the entire existence.[1]

- Jesus said, "I and the Father are one,"[2] "Whoever believes in me will do the works I have been doing, and they will do even greater things than these,"[3] "The Kingdom of God is in your

---

1. Li, Er (Lao Zi (Lao Tzu)). *Dao De Jing* (Tao Te Ching). Translated as *Laozi's Classic of the Way and the Virtue*. c.500 BCE to 101 BCE.

midst,"[4] and "that all of them may be one, Father, just as you are in me and I am in you. May they also be in us."[5] All of these refer to the oneness of all.

- Buddha spoke of simply *being*.[6] He also spoke much of love—unconditional love.[7]

Finally, the essence of almost all religions is the notion of faith—faith in their interpretation of what God is. Faith itself is a useful tool because it allows humans to believe in something grander than their current self. It allows

---

4. Luke 17:21. *The Bible*. New International Version. Often cited as "The Kingdom of God is within you."

5. John 17:21. *The Bible*. New International Version.

humans to form a belief and state of being that is the grandest version of who they are. This allows for progress and transformation, for only when one sees oneself in a certain way does reality catch up to that vision.

CHAPTER 8

Where science replaced religion

As humans naturally progressed technologically, new observations about the world around us delivered new information about biology, geology, cosmology, and physics that increased science's contradictions with religious texts and amplified the internal contradictions within religious texts. Religion, in its pursuit of absolute faith in truth, can be said to have confused faith in truth with faith in text.

Science, on the other hand, has its foundation rooted in the scientific process. By this very nature, science questions, debunks, and creates itself anew whenever new information and understanding come to light. This practice of constant renewal of understanding is not only consistent with natural human understanding and growth (think of common sense or the curiosity of children asking why things work), it is the very essence of human existence—to create ourselves anew each moment of every day.

Gradually, religions that cannot adapt and change their beliefs start to lose credibility. It is like listening to someone who cannot do simple arithmetic explain how best to run a restaurant. Although it is possible and plausible that someone who cannot do math can run a restaurant extremely well. But the messages this particular person discusses about a restaurant's financial models would be significantly discounted by anyone with common sense who cares about the credibility of the messenger as much as the message itself. If religion is a system of beliefs about truth, among which is the truth about God, then facilitators of religion better have some credibility about the very basic workings of the "seeable" part of life that is beyond contestation to make us believe the other truths that are "unseeable" by common standards, such as "God."

Yes, I understand that a key component of religion is faith, and a devout religious middle school classmate of mine once elegantly defined "faith" for me as "believing without seeing." But believing can have degrees, and our beliefs should be free to change when new information comes to light that proves or disproves (with certain probabilities) our prior beliefs.

Religion, on the other hand, does not seem to allow us to evolve like the rest of life and the rest of our human experience. That which does not evolve is easily rendered obsolete because life itself is "change." The only constant in the cosmos is change.

CHAPTER 9

Where science failed

W here science started to falter (or at least many people's incomplete view of science) is first and foremost *faith*. Here, I do not mean blind faith without question but a leap of faith. Many people who claim that they believe in science and not God speak of the requirement for proof as the definitive truth. But they forget that even the scientific process, which most of these people embrace, often starts with a hypothesis that is just a conjecture—in other words, a belief about the world that is yet to be proven. Even many theories that we hold as truths are going to always be called theories because they are simply that: one explanation of how and why things are, but never the only explanation. Most certainly, theories do not profess to be the truth but instead an attempt at describing the truth.

Furthermore, true scientists understand that scientific laws are not infallible either. Laws describe what is, but only from a limited human vantage point. Science now understands that the process of observation itself influences what is observed. In the absence of any objective way to describe anything, science has often been open-minded enough to say, "We do not have proof, but we can still believe what is so, given the limited understanding that we have today." Then by that logic, can science accept that "God" is part of a particular scientific theory and believe such theory to be true before it is proven false? We all know the common wisdom that an absence of proof is not proof of absence. Such faith that science lacks is the leap of faith that religion at least attempts to do and even embraces. It is the blind faith and staunch attachment to old information that religion has failed, but not the original thesis (or theory) of God.

Many scientists who believed in God, such as Albert Einstein, understood this.

One conversation in the movie *Contact*, which is based on Carl Sagan's novel of the same name, was a lighthearted demonstration of a discussion on faith. When the SETI scientist, Dr. Ellie Arroway, discussed God with Minister Palmer Joss, Ellie commented, "Occam's razor...says, all things being equal, the simplest explanation tends to be the right one." She continued, "So what's more likely...an all-powerful mysterious God created the universe and decided not to give any proof of its existence, or that he simply doesn't exist at all and that we created him so that we wouldn't have to feel so small and alone." To that, Palmer replied, "I don't know. I cannot imagine a world where God didn't exist. I wouldn't want to". Ellie then asked, "How do you know you're not deluding yourself? For me, I need proof." Palmer pondered for a moment, "Proof..." Then he turned and asked Ellie, "Did you love your father? Your Dad, did you love him?" Ellie responded, "Yes, very much." Palmer then asked simply, "Prove it."

Ask yourself this question about many things you hold as absolutely true, and you may find that you, too, would be lost for words. Many things in life are simply not provable, at least not convincing beyond a shadow of a doubt.

The biggest failure of science and religion has been the misuse of them by those in power which caused profound human suffering. Science as a tool, much like religion, can be and has been used in history as a means to control, suppress, and oppress, and has been misused for monetary gains for the furtherance of power and control. For instance, using science to sway public opinion about certain health benefits or drawbacks of certain food ingredients has been the ploy for many users of such manipulation to shift public opinion about one foodstuff for monetary gains.

The powerful demonstration of the scientific process has also rendered itself a dangerous tool from time to time. Much like using the power of God in religions to instill fear as a mechanism of control, science, too, can be an effective tool to instill fear and doubt for the purpose of manipulation precisely because it is so believable and authoritative, just like God once was in the days of religion.

CHAPTER 10

Where science and religion meet

Perhaps the one thing we can do is first bless both science and religion and honor them for their true purpose and original intent. We can express gratitude that both are human attempts to arrive at truth. Starting from this vantage point, we see that neither science nor religion is inherently good or bad for us. It is the application of each that leads us to directions that either serve us or not, depending on where we want to go as a species. If where we want to go is the manipulation of others for our personal gains, both science and religion are great tools to achieve that. If where we want to go is arriving at the truth, at least both make earnest attempts to do so. The key ingredient is an earnest attempt to arrive at the truth and be willing first to acknowledge that our knowledge of the existence around us is like the existence itself, forever changing as new information comes to light while having the leap of faith and audacity to believe in what we know as true, whether the tangible proof is available to us or not at this current state of our understanding. That is the hallmark of being authentic.

In truth, it does not matter whether one believes in science or religion, or is an atheist, agnostic, theist, or of any religious affiliation. The truth simply *is*—no matter what people believe. Conversely, whether a belief is ultimately true or not is unimportant in the absolute sense, for the purpose of any belief is its usefulness in allowing us to shape ourselves or communicate what we believe is true to ourselves and others. As long as we honor our choice and the pursuit of truth, the journey of adopting and dropping any belief is meaningful in and of itself in our human experience.

Chapter 11

Oneness

For most atheists, there is no one else but humans or the self (or individual selves). Some do not believe in any non-Earth-originated entities, such as intelligent life on other planets, let alone entities of a higher power. This belief system may seem as far away from the notion of "God" as possible. However, in some regards, it is closer to the absolute spiritual truth than many religions profess to embrace.

When you believe there is no one else (instead of the existence of a God that punishes us), you only have to take the small step of knowing the connectedness of all there is to come to the conclusion that "you" are all that is. You simply then have to expand your definition of "self" to get to the possible notion that *you* and other people on this planet are perhaps not separate; perhaps all people and animals and the planet are not separate; then, at last, you may accept the notion that the entire cosmos is one connected "thing."

This concept of Oneness, albeit simple, is difficult for many people to accept. We can be made of the same stuff, but it is more difficult to see the individuated "you" being connected to other human beings, let alone animals, trees, water, and other stars and planets.

Here is where a leap of faith comes in and is the bridge to ultimate truth. For now, I only suggest that you suspend your beliefs and assume for the time being that the concept of Oneness is the ultimate truth of all of existence.

In the following chapters, I will outline what can happen in our world if an increasing number of people believe the concept of Oneness and act in accordance with that belief system, as well as all other corollaries derived from this truth. You can decide in the end what you choose to believe.

CHAPTER 12

Implications of Oneness

WHAT CAN HAPPEN WHEN WE ADOPT THE BELIEF OF ONENESS?

Regardless of the truth, what you believe in does not have to be the truth or may not necessarily *be* the truth. Sometimes, from certain perspectives, the truth does not matter. To use a simple example, we still say the sun rises and the sun sets, make poetry and paintings about sunrise and sunsets because of their sheer beauty, knowing full well (most of us anyway) that the sun neither rises nor sets in absolute terms[1]. There-fore, you can know the absolute truth of the cosmos in regard to the sun and planets but still choose to use the phrases "sunrise" or "sunset" to communicate the practical timeframe of the day or express the phenom-enon in poetic terms instead of scientific terms.

I say this here because what I am about to discuss in terms of Oneness is what I believe to be the truth. But if it is difficult for you to accept without a shadow of a doubt, I suggest that that is okay, too. You may still behold its beauty, benefit from its practical uses, and a-ffect your life and the lives of others by pretending it is true. As long as it serves you for a purpose that pleases you, what does it matter whether it is an absolute truth or not?

---

1. A similar reference was made in *A New Earth: Awakening to Your Life's Purpose* by Eckhart Tolle. Tolle, Eckhart (2005). *A New Earth: Awakening to Your Life's Purpose*. Plume.

The implication of believing in the Oneness of All is that we diminish the fundamental source of all of our problems in the world—one that originates from a sense of separation. We could get to the understanding of Oneness from many directions. I will demonstrate it in a few ways.

Sense of self

From economics to theology, we see a narrow concept of "self" throughout human endeavors.

Economic concepts, such as individuals aiming to maximize their utility or happiness, are concepts that most people can accept. We can see that the notion of self in these economic models is a rather narrow one.

Similarly, in biology, the Darwinian theory of evolution, though focused on an entire species' survival, still describes each individual member of the species as self-preserving.

Common phrases such as "every man for himself," "survival of the fittest" (as used for individualistic nature, not Darwinian species context), and "the personal is the political" all show our human understanding of a world based on a narrow definition of self.

Expansion of the "self"

We will take economics as an example, as it appears less relevant to spiritual matters and can allow us a further removed perspective for enhanced clarity. Most people, religious or not, tend to agree with certain economic theories, so it is a good starting point for the discussion around the "self."

Economics uses the concept of maximizing the utility or happiness of an individual as a model for our society or at least our economic system. If our wider society functions in a way where individuals maximize the utility or happiness of the "self," it may appear that altruism and sacrifice for the greater good and other desirable behaviors that benefit the masses at the expense of the individual become something unattainable. On the other hand, such sacrifices are no doubt desirable by society as a whole because they create the greater good.

One solution here is the adoption of the spiritual concept of Oneness by people, to whatever degree, to essentially widen the definition of "self." We can easily see this anecdotally from the selfless acts of parents toward their children, and we can explain that the parents simply widened their sense of self to include their offspring as an extension of themselves. This inclusiveness can apply to the wider family, tribe, nation, entire civilization, entire planetary-bio system, and beyond. It is only a matter of perspective of the self and how connected the self believes it to be with the rest of existence.

Therefore, the implication of more individuals embracing the notion that they are connected to each other, their surroundings, and the entire extended system is that we can come to understand that what is done to others is done to ourselves. All the actions driven by self-interest are therefore reconciled when All is One because what is good for "others" is good for the "self." When this self includes all of humanity, we cease to have wars. When this self includes the entire biosphere, we naturally take care of our environment.

This does not mean we do not eat living things (plants included) or cut down any trees. It means we consider the system as a whole and consider the greater good.

Conversely, it would also be prudent to consider the consequence of impunity of any action, namely, the logic that if I am only doing it to myself anyway, what difference does it make? I can kill as I wish and destroy the environment if it pleases me. To this argument, we go back to the notion that Oneness means whatever is done to others is done to the self. As with any single system, it will naturally come to an action pattern consistent with harmony within the self.

By adopting this belief of unity of All, we expand our definition of self for the practical implication of greater harmony.

Sufficiency

Another implication of Oneness is sufficiency. No doubt, we currently live in a paradigm based on lack and insufficiency.

We govern ourselves with decisions based on economics that speak of scarcity and supply and demand as the supreme law and natural law that governs human activities. We, therefore, hoard natural resources instead of sharing equitably, demonstrating that we have a mindset of lack.

When we embrace Oneness instead of a paradigm of scarcity, we see other people as part of us, naturally rendering a generosity of spirit. Furthermore, we will then share freely and love others because we understand that what we do to others, we do unto ourselves. It would be self-serving and practical to take care of other people. Natural resources will be seen as abundant, but not in a way where we abuse them. When shared naturally, and that is in our true nature of love to share equitably, what we have is enough for our current state of being because we will eliminate the need for supply and demand distortions to maintain inflated prices and hoard resources.

Additionally, by adopting the belief of Oneness, we eliminate the need for the arms race, which is the biggest sink of our natural and economic resources. When we recognize that we are all one, there is no need for war, hence no need for arms buildup. Of course, practically, I recognize that from where we are now to the state that most of us embrace Oneness as the truth, the transition phase requires steady advancements in multiple areas and growth in spiritual awareness to make our human evolution gradual and comfortable for everyone. The hypothesis of such transition mechanisms is beyond the scope of this book. My personal hypothesis and vision of how that transition might be is irrelevant to the truth of Oneness I am describing here. Changing mindset and belief by adopting the concept of Oneness can nonetheless create our collective desired outcome of peace, prosperity, wisdom, and bliss as a human race.

Forgiveness

When you see others as an extension of yourself, it would be easier to forgive the behavior of others who appear to have hurt you. As one experiences a greater sense of internalizing oneness in all aspects of life, one will inevitably find that forgiveness is not necessary because others cannot hurt you at the soul level or the level of your true identity, which is one with all. Because, in essence, there is nothing to forgive and no one else to forgive. We may still use apology and forgiveness as an expression of our love for others, especially toward those who may not have the same understanding or level of understanding of oneness as we do. Forgiveness and apology, then, are simply acts of compassion expressed in a way that is helpful for the other person, though not necessary in the absolute sense.

When we recognize this, we can still choose to function in our society and act out our kindness and compassion toward others (in essence, other selves) by forgiving others while recognizing that other people are simply extensions of us and that forgiveness is not truly necessary.

Creation and manifestation

When we recognize the Oneness of All, we also see the secret of creation and the creative process. In our current existence as sentient beings on Earth, we truly create our own reality, not just through thought but through our being.

In essence, though, we are creating nothing because all that ever is, was, and will be, and all combinations and permutations thereof already exist in the single perfect moment of now. We simply call forth the experience which we desire. This is drastically different from traditional schools of thought on manifestation, where "thoughts become things" and we manifest through our thoughts alone or we actively create things and events into existence.

When we recognize our Oneness with All, which transcends our limited understanding of time, the extension of self includes all possible versions of the self and other selves and all things and events. This knowing is so powerful in manifesting your own experience that it unlocks all possibilities for you. Indeed, when you *are* that which you desire, the universe aligns itself to deliver that exact experience to you effortlessly because that experience already exists—as part of you.

The construct of time

Given what we discussed about the infinite possible versions of *all that is* already exist in the perfect moment of now, what, then, is *time*? Time is the mechanism by which we have created our absolute existence so that we can enjoy the process of choice and experience that which we desire to experience. It is like watching a movie. We watch movies by frames, and not all at once, for the pure enjoyment of it.

Various versions of the current scientific understanding of quantum physics support some notion of this singular moment of time and everlasting and eternal moment of now, housing all the infinite possibilities of everything. Though at the present moment (in the practical sense, not in the spiritual, esoteric senses of this phrase), even true believers of science have a hard time accepting the latest theories about space and time because they run so counter to our conventional understanding of time that even render the theory of relativity obsolete. It would be helpful to be reminded that in our recent human history, we have accepted Newtonian theory of gravity as absolute truth for centuries before Einstein's theory of relativity replaced Newtonian theory. By this measure, it is not a stretch that these newer theories will someday replace the theory of relativity and be adopted as the then predominant beliefs until yet another new understanding occurs.

Everything is an illusion

Once we see that time does not truly exist as we traditionally understand it, the next logical conclusion is understanding that everything is an illusion.

From the perspective of physics, we can glimpse a practical version of this understanding by using our scientific finding that everything is made of the same stuff—atoms. "Matter," whether it is people, plants, rocks, or water, is all made of atoms arranged in a particular formation. However, when you look at matter up close, there is more space than actual substance in any matter. In essence, we are made up more of "nothing" than "something." To take it one step further, electrons and photons exist as probabilistic waves. Only when someone observes them do electrons and photons appear as particles or, in a sense, "come into existence." I am over-simplifying, of course, but this perspective is sufficient providing one perspective in the understanding of illusion.

Consider these observations merely as glimpses of the true nature of our reality in that there appears to be some intangible quality to what we accept as unmoving facts, such as *matter* that we can touch, feel, and see. If we combine these observations about *matter* with what we discussed about time and infinite possibilities, it is easier to accept the possibility that our reality as we know it can better be described as an illusion.

The acceptance of the concept of illusion can serve us well in our daily lives by not being attached to any particular outcome and rendering everything that comes to pass as something transient. Only in accepting this concept of illusion can we care deeply and live passionately in the moment without fear. We cease to have fear because we know that it is not possible for us to suffer true loss and that because everything is an illusion, it is possible to understand that we can mold and create the illusion for our pure enjoyment. This lighthearted attitude is one way to experience the joy of being and non-attachment. We can still have desires and choose our experience, but we do not have to be disheartened by any particular happening—because we can always change the illusion.

The purpose of the illusion – the contextual field

What is the purpose of the illusion? In the beginning, there is only unity. Everything was a single point of nothingness. We can call this state "the realm of the absolute."

In this realm of the absolute, all is perfection; it is not possible to know "evil" or experience "forgiveness" because no one is ever hurt, and there is nothing and no one else to forgive. Indeed, there is no one else, but the *Everything That Is* is nothing but one thing. In other words, the *Everything That Is* in existence is incomplete in its experience because although it knows of itself as *everything that is*, it cannot know this truth experientially. Therefore, the *Everything That Is* created the grand illusion of separateness so that part of itself may experience something that it is not. Because "in the absence of that which is not, that which is, is not,"[2] meaning, "in the absence of 'cold,' 'hot' is not." One cannot know "high" without "low" being a contextual field on which to experience "high." One cannot know "good" if there is no "bad" as a contextual field to experience "good." In the absence of that which is not love, "love" is not. Therefore, the Everything created separateness and illusions of a relative realm so that part of itself may experience love by creating the seeming antithesis of love so that it can experience everything else in between, including "forgiveness."

The illusion, then, makes it possible for infinite contextual fields in which everything can be known experientially through the juxtaposition between opposites. The entire existence is now complete.

In truth, this all happens in no time. All that ever is has existed and always will be in existence. The All of It was,

---

2. Walsch, Neale Donald (2005). *Conversations with God: An Uncommon Dialogue Book I, Book II and Book III*. Phoenix Books.

in fact, complete since inception (and there was never an inception).

Fundamental building blocks of all existence

If All is an illusion, what makes up this grand illusion? What is the fundamental building block of the universe or our entire existence? I offer one perspective that the answer can best be described as "love." Love is all that is. By this love, I mean the absolute sense of the concept and not simply carnal love or a substitute for "like," implying preferences. Some spiritual teachers explain this "love" as "pure love" for clearer and easier understanding. I believe this is useful, but I am often reminded that love is love, and love is already the purest essence. We can debate about the definition and nuances, which would all be valid because our human language is perhaps inadequate in describing this truth. Alternatively, we could replace "love" with "essence" and still serve the same purpose of understanding. But using the word "love" has profound practical implications.

Love is all that is

Using *love* to describe the essence that makes up life and everything there is has profound practical implications. We humans intuitively and instinctively honor "love" as the highest form of emotion or feeling in almost all cultures, modern or historical. If we can take one step further in describing all emotions or feelings as derivatives of love, we then have an even more profound way of understanding human behavior and the workings of the universe.

Consider the greatest hurt that anyone can suffer at the hands of another. We might describe such acts as derivatives of the feeling or emotion that we call "hate." We may also traditionally explain hate as the absence of "love" or the antithesis of love. But I offer another perspective you may find useful and accept as your truth if it serves you.

What if we consider all emotions as being derived from love? Test this concept in your daily life and historical context. I personally find that when I ask myself this single question, "What does the person love so much that they are willing to do what they are doing to this other person?",[3] I can gain unparalleled clarity in the situation and find compassion and understanding in all situations I encounter.

I do not always transcend my emotional understanding, but I can see how this transcendence is possible through this question. I do not always confront the person with the question, but a hypothetical conversation in my head is often sufficient for me to arrive at an understanding that is helpful to me. Whether the person would agree with my simulated conversation if they had the chance to answer this question in reality or whether the person

---

3. A form of this question was suggested in the *Conversations with God*. Walsch, Neale Donald (2005). *Conversations with God: An Uncommon Dialogue Book I, Book II and Book III*. Phoenix Books.

even knows the true answer to this question becomes irrelevant.

The meaning of life

We now come full circle to the fundamental human question: what is the meaning of all this? What is the meaning of life and our existence?

I offer this: the meaning of life is the pure experience of it. In essence, the meaning of anything is the meaning you give it. You *are* in control, though sometimes it may not feel like it in our current existence. But in the absolute sense of who you truly are, you give anything its meaning. Therefore, you give life its meaning. In the absolute sense, life is choosing the experience and being that experience. When it pleases you, make another choice and experience that.

Another way of looking at the meaning of our existence is "to be the grandest version of the greatest vision you ever held for yourself."[4] I have come to understand my life's purpose, which I define as "just be, just create." Of course, given what we discussed earlier, what I mean by "create" is simply choosing the experience which has, in the absolute sense, already been created.

There is no "good versus evil"

Combining this understanding with the understanding that love is all there is, life can be understood as the expression of love, no matter what comes to pass. This is a powerful concept to embrace, particularly when thinking about the age-old question of the meaning of life. Often, people ask, "What is the meaning of life?" when they confront experiences of horrendous human suffering. Their question can almost be rephrased as "Why is

---

4. Walsch, Neale Donald (2005). *Conversations with God: An Uncommon Dialogue Book I, Book II and Book III*. Phoenix Books.

life so meaningless?" If we truly understand that love is all there is, then we understand that nothing is *not* an expression of love and can come to an understanding that we serve the greater purpose of the expression of love no matter what happens, whether we are supposedly the perpetrator or the victim.

This concept is the most difficult for most people to embrace, whether staunch atheists, devout religious people, or spiritually inclined. We are so entrenched in our human experience—the concept of right and wrong, absolute morality, and the larger social construct of social norms—that we believe it is normal to reject the notion that everything is pure and that there must be, in absolute terms, certain things, behaviors, people, places, and events that are inherently evil or "bad."

This concept, ironically, is perhaps precisely why many atheists can still act morally and ethically without subscribing to the fear of a so-called God. Perhaps because our true human nature is love and that fear of negative consequences is not essential for us to produce "good" behavior. We are loving simply because we *are* love.

Life never ends

If we are All and all is One, then we are life itself, and therefore, we have always existed and always shall exist. It then follows that life never ends, and we must never die. Another way of putting it is that death is an illusion.

This is the single most liberating implication of the Oneness system of belief because the most debilitating emotion in human existence has been fear, and most of all, fear of death. Without this fear of death, then nothing in comparison to death is such a big deal that cannot be overcome. A life without fear is a life of joy, bliss, and eternality.

In short, we do not die but simply change form. However, some people may point out that it is all well and good to say that the elements that make up "me" always exist. But if my existence is reduced to a pile of ashes or some disintegrated energy, the "me," for all practical and recognizable purposes as a conscious existence no longer is, I would still be *practically* dead. So to say we simply change form is an impractical and undesirable way of looking at death and eternal life.

To that point, I wholeheartedly agree with the logic and rebuttal. I, therefore, offer the belief that the consciousness that gives us our existence recognizable meaning and practical purpose truly exists beyond what we commonly call "death."

Putting it all together:

If we go back to where we began the discussion of "Oneness" all the way to "love being all there is", we have a complete belief system with practical uses and implications. You see, in this system of belief, nothing is *not* derived from "love," and though it may be difficult to accept or believe this concept, you can see the simplistic beauty of this point of view of the universe if not for the simple, practical reason of gaining a perspective by which no matter what happens, you can be in a state of understanding, compassion, and purpose. Even if the concept turns out not to be the absolute truth of reality, I choose to embrace it now because I prefer to let this perspective guide me to see love in everything, even the direst of situations.

CHAPTER 13

Atheism and God

This is finally the place where we will revisit the notion of God and how some atheists do not believe in the existence of God as religions define God or in any higher power whatsoever.

Indeed, when I ask most atheists why they do not believe in God, I find that most atheists simply reject the notion of a God that behaves as humans do—having a sense of punishment, a need for allegiance from humans, and a tendency to demonstrate power. These qualities seem so trivial and imperfect that they are certainly more likely projections of humans and, in a sense, support the belief that humans created God. It follows that many atheists first and foremost reject the anthropomorphism portion of religions and religions' scope of God, where God exemplifies all human qualities.

The only difference, then, between what I call spiritualism and atheism, is simply their definitions of God. If you ask an atheist, "Does life exist?" an atheist would likely say, "Yes, of course." Life itself, whatever the atheist chooses to believe the definition of "life" to be, is an "*isness*", which is just the way it is. If, then, we say that we scrap the concept of God completely and adopt a concept around "life", then an atheist, or almost everyone on Earth, can agree that life happens. If the study of life is spirituality, and people who adopt a belief about certain workings of life are called spiritualists, then everyone can be deemed a spiritualist under that particular definition and framework.

It begs the question, is spiritualism or spirituality even necessary? We then seem to go back to some form of anthropocentrism—humans being the central or most important element of existence—rather than God or nature. This idea of anthropocentrism and other atheist schools of thought appear to be on one end of the spectrum in the belief of a God of any kind while spirituality and religion appear to be on the other end of the spectrum. However, a different perspective can point to a surprisingly different kind of truth: Perhaps atheism is closer to spirituality than most think.

Ye *are* God

If "you" (we, humans) are all that there is, and the "you" is the largest, expanded definition of one connected "thing", then "you" must be what religions call God. You are not only God's extension; you are God's equal. You *are* God, and not just "gods," as in the case of any entity less than God, because, in essence, we are all One. We are one with each other, and if there is only One, then that One must be God. If the word "God" has too much religious baggage, we can replace the word "God" with "love" or "life" and arrive at the same conclusion. You are *love*. You are *life*.

Such revelation ironically becomes consistent with an atheist's human-centric belief of anthropocentrism, but not in a conceited, unloving way where humans are the center of the universe and, therefore, command and subvert everything else. It is based on the oneness of it all and that "All" is all that there is. If "All" is "One," then even by selfish human logic, that One must be forever loving to all parts of itself, then love is indeed all that there is. And if everything is one, then there is nothing that is not One, and therefore, all that *ever was, ever is,* and *ever will be* already exist as part of that One.

Very few religions teach us this truth or would be willing to have the leap of faith or even the benefit of the doubt that this belief may be possible. They continue to hold the notion that God is somehow separate from us despite original spiritual teachings to the contrary.

At least science, at its most cutting-edge discovery, accepts many aspects of the workings of our universe that are consistent with "oneness" without giving it the name "God."

Even if you define God as a being, an energy, a totality, something that is conscious or sentient, even having human qualities, as long as you believe that such an existence is love or the absolute expression of love, then I would have the audacity to say that this God does not mind at all whether you believe in the existence of God. This God that is all-powerful cannot be hurt, so there is no need for God to be angry at anything, including your belief or lack of belief in God's existence. If God is all-powerful and perfect, then God must be able to have anything happen the way God intends, and therefore, if God intends for anyone believing in the existence of God as some sort of requirement, would not God be able to get God's way without fail? Or is God such a lesser god that God is capable of failure? Somehow, even by the standard of most religions, such a lesser view of God seems blasphemous. We could, therefore, safely conclude that the current state is as God intended. And if that means a state in which some people hold the belief in no God, then such state is also God's will. Therefore, the question of whether God exists becomes irrelevant.

What is the implication of this line of logic? We can focus on our own spirituality and live life's essence without the need to debate about God's existence or fear of "getting it wrong." One can believe or deny God's existence and still be "enlightened" because as long as one accepts what the ultimate truth is, what God is or is not, simply *is*. In the end, we are only left to debate what God really is. If God is simply the totality of everything, love, or life itself, then what is there to debate about?

Your own belief

All I have done so far in this book is humbly present one belief system and offer practical applications of it so that others simply see the benefit of adopting some or part of it. Even if these concepts are not absolute truths, we can decide now that it does not matter. Because, like the words "sunset" and "sunrise," the concept of Oneness communicates a way of life clearly and concisely and allows us to create beautiful poetries of love in our lives.

This notion that it does not matter whether an ideology is true or not, as long as it is practical, may ironically be one reason religions adopted the notion of an angry and punishing God—because they may have had the loving motivation of getting people to do the "right" thing, albeit in accordance to their own standards and by largely deploying the tool of fear.

So long as the Oneness can lead us to a life that is compassionate and loving and creates a planetary shift that provides us with a version of the Earth's future that most people desire, then the concept is worth being widely adopted as our new paradigm or, dare I say, religion. Rather than calling it anything, I choose to call this paradigm spirituality, with the most generic definition that spirituality is simply about life itself.

You have your own truths that you hold dear. Perhaps that truth is in the religion you follow, the nation-state to which you pledge allegiance, or the family you see as the core of your existence that you seek to defend against all else in the world. That is okay. This belief of Oneness is about inclusion, not exclusion. Indeed, it is impossible for your belief to fall outside of the Oneness because the One is all that is!

Your own belief system may evolve if it pleases you or stay as is as another beautiful piece of the tapestry of life. In fact, when more and more people adopt Oneness as their belief in their state of being, the different views create welcomed diversity, not division. We will love each other more fully for our differences, even those who choose to still believe in our separation as the truth.

Those who believe and experience Oneness will experience love and joy. For those who remain identified with the great illusions, we can still use the illusion as the greatest gift for us to play in this reality and create (choose) our particular blend of experiences.

We bless each moment, the eternal moment of now, with joy and fulfillment. We savor the moments that we remember our purpose in life, and we treasure the moments that we forget so that we can act as if we are children enjoying our own drama in order to laugh and cry with the strongest and purest expressions of love.

What, then, do you choose to believe now?

About the author
Peter Ahkia

Peter Ahkia lives in Vancouver, British Colum-
bia. Growing up in a family with very little religious faith or affiliation, his view of the world had
always been from a secular, scientific, and humanist
perspective. It was not until he visited Europe in the
1990s that he expressed a profound interest in religion,
starting with the history of Christianity and the wider
effect religion has on architecture, art, and human evolution. Born in Asia and having lived in the Middle
East as a child, Peter Ahkia innocently incorporated elements of Christianity, Buddhism, Daoism, and Islam
into his prayers as an adolescent.

Peter Ahkia's spiritual path did not come in a single moment of awakening or epiphany, but in short spurts of chance encounters, serendipities, and simple, almost imperceptible shifts.

During his trip to Italy as an 11-year-old, he recalls writing in his school journal about an experience that some Catholics would describe as stigmata—having a mark appear on his body that resembled the wounds of Jesus as Jesus went through crucifixion. Peter Ahkia now explains the experience as possibly a case of a child's outstanding imagination with influences from seeing so much religious art for the first time in his life. His younger self was not aware that the phenomenon of stigmata was reported to exist nor did he know the meaning or religious significance of stigmata at the time.

The experience did inspire young Peter Ahkia to formulate a blended method of prayers sourced from multiple religious practices that he knew at the time. His university years, by contrast, was marked by conscious avoidance of any religious affiliation whatsoever. The period was dominated by social life, exploration of political science, biology, psychology, but, ultimately, a focus on business and entrepreneurship with little to do with spirituality or religion. It was not until he was back in Europe, in London, UK, working as an investment banker, that he resumed his old practice of quiet contemplation and private prayers directly to God, albeit only lasting a few years.

A decade passed since he departed London, worked in Asia, returned to his second hometown Vancouver, and encountered the works for Eckhart Tolle, who, incidentally, was also a Vancouver resident. Tolle's work inspired Peter Ahkia to revisit religion and spirituality, ranging from esoteric metaphysical works and practices to Kriya Yoga of the same tradition as Paramahansa Yogananda, who followed the lineage of Sri Yukteswar and Lahiri Mahasaya. Peter Ahkia also studied with Neale Donald Walsch (author of Conversations with God), among other spiritual peers.

Peter Ahkia founded the Ahkia Institute of Spiritual Studies and continues to serve seekers of truth to this day.

www.ahkia.com

Thank you

Stay connected

T hank you for spending the time with me and my work. I would very much like to hear from you and stay in touch. You can do any of the following:

1. You can email me directly at one@ahkia.com. I will reply to all emails and you will be added to my email list.

2. I would also encourage you to leave a book review on goodreads.com to get a free eBook from me (let me know by email).

Reviews are important to an author. Your review will be greatly appreciated. If you email me to let me know that you have posted a review on goodreads.com, I will gift you the digital version of my next book that will be published on February 20, 2024 on the topic of spiritual parenting or the book after that on advanced spiritual concepts, which will be published on April 23, 2024.

You can also visit www.ahkia.com (the Ahkia Institute website) for further resources, schedule one-on-one sessions with me, or download the Spiritual Money™ app for free guided meditations and more.